Contents

1 First take off the
nightdress.

2 Then put the underwear on.

shift

3 Next put on her stockings, garters and shoes.

garters

silk stockings

high-heeled silk shoes

4 Pull the laces of her corset tight.

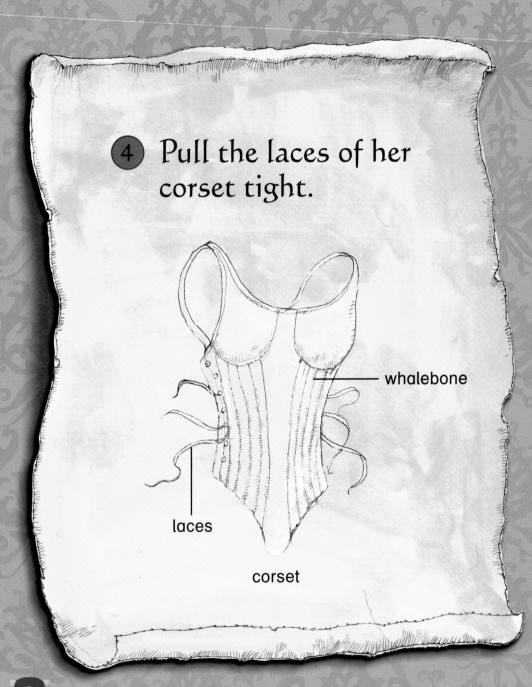

whalebone

laces

corset

5 Now fix the frame around her waist.

wire

farthingale

6 Put on her petticoats and skirts.

silk petticoats

skirt

7 Then put on her top.

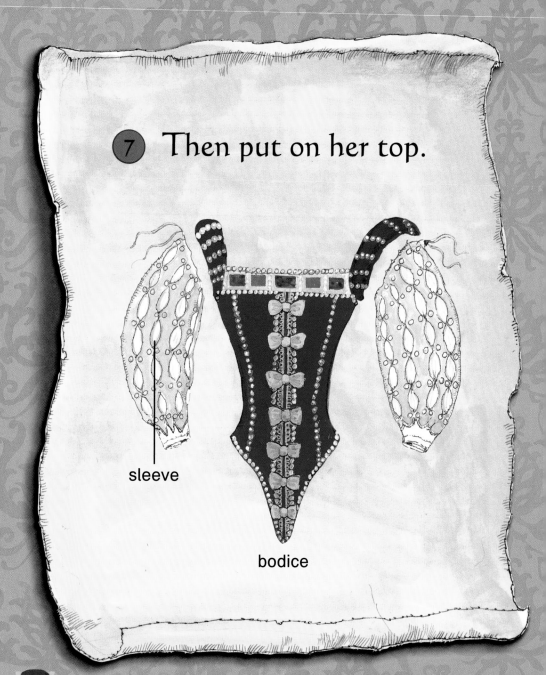

sleeve

bodice

8 Fix the collars around her neck.

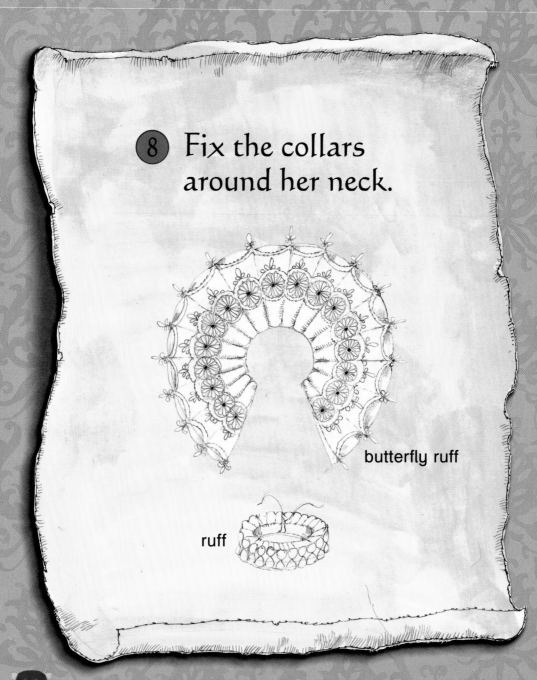

butterfly ruff

ruff

9 Now put on her jewels.

pendant

pomander
(sweet-smelling)

10 Finally, put on her earrings and wig.

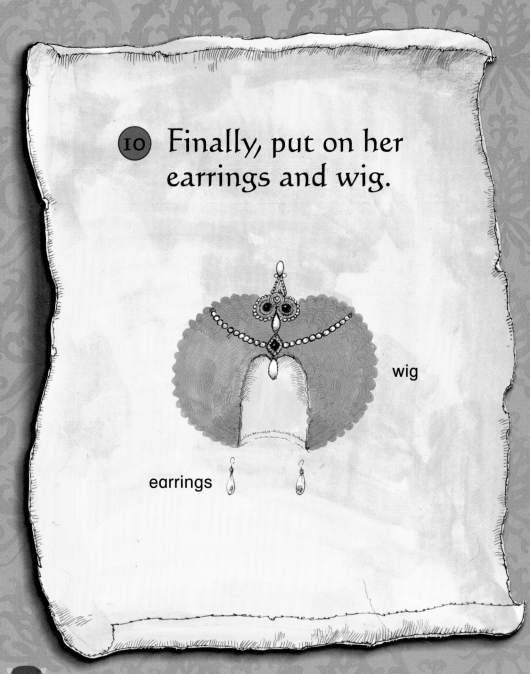

wig

earrings

What you need

sleeve

bodice

pendant

wig

butterfly ruff

corset

earrings

ruff

shift

pomander
(sweet-smelling)

high-heeled
silk shoes

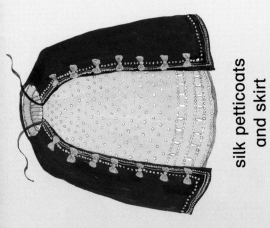

silk petticoats
and skirt

garters

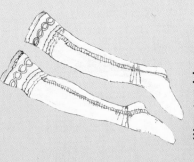

silk stockings

farthingale

Index